The
Greatest
Gift

*Finding 100 blessings from
the Fort McMurray
Wild Fire*

JOY ELLEN LALONDE

◆ FriesenPress

Suite 300 - 990 Fort St
Victoria, BC, V8V 3K2
Canada

www.friesenpress.com

ISBN
978-1-5255-0197-5 (Hardcover)
978-1-5255-0198-2 (Paperback)
978-1-5255-0199-9 (eBook)

1. Religion, Christian Life, Inspirational

Distributed to the trade by The Ingram Book Company

It is my intention to illustrate that out of every situation
there are blessings and only good can come.
I wish to reach as many people as I can to share
that Feeling blessed is so much Better
than feeling Burdened.
The choice is yours.

Let's Be Free
Let's Be Blessed

I dedicate this book to all of the people affected by the
Fort McMurray Wild Fire. May you find inner peace,
comfort and many blessings of your own.

'Joy comes from within.'

In Appreciation

I would like to thank my best friend and amazing daughter Ali Lynne. The insight she has shown me over the years is overwhelming. To my handsome son Tate Joseph thank you for making me laugh and showing me unconditional faith in a higher power. To Daren Lalonde to whom I get to share my life with. I truly appreciate your love and support in all that I do. I am blessed.

Thank you to The Bridge Babes who continue to inspire and guide me to inner joy. This unique group of ladies have taught me the meaning of *UNCONDITIONAL* and for that I am extremely blessed.

A special thank you to my mom and Aunt Mary,
who encouraged me to publish my blessings.
To Emily MacDonald, my 'Happy Accident' and the
entire staff at Friesen Press, your support and faith in
my book has been a blessing to me. Thank you.
I am extremely grateful.

In loving memory of my dad who always
told me to "Go For It"

Well dad, I did. Thanks

Preface

Close your eyes.
Take a deep breathe in.
Hold it for four seconds.

As you exhale, imagine yourself driving down a highway, walls of fire raging on both sides. You've hastily packed one suitcase and tossed as many valuables into your vehicle as you could.

Little do you know, this is all you will have from your home for the next few months, perhaps forever.

Please, keep this in mind as you read the following blessing posts. These blessings arose within the first few weeks of evacuation during an uncertain, chaotic, frustrating, and fearful time. In this dark hour, the blessings shone bright and warmed my heart. I hope they do the same for you.

The
Greatest
Gift

CHAPTER 1

Evacuation Day

Tuesday May 3, 2016, a day in history that many Fort McMurray residents will not soon forget. It was a day filled with panic, disbelief, order and disorder. A community coming together to safely evacuate people, pets and prized possessions.

Heroism, selflessness and inner strength shone brightly. We were blessed.

Everyone has his or her own unique story and tales of leaving the burning city. I enjoyed listening to people recounting their escape. A common theme throughout was how overwhelming the support was in Alberta and around the world. It seemed like for a moment in time, the world came together to help a small Northern city, in Alberta Canada through a crisis.

CHAPTER 2

Half empty or half full: You have a choice

Surrounded by flames and smoke with very little visibility, my heart sank and for a split second my faith crumbled. I closed my eyes and said to myself "this is not how I am going to die!" Minutes after my declaration, the flames drew back, the smoke lifted and we were soon driving down Highway 63 as if nothing devastating was happening . Unbelievable. I knew at that moment that I had to find the good or 'Blessings' in all of this. So my mission began.

I chose half full.

CHAPTER 3

The
Blessings

One by one the blessings started to trickle in. I declared to my daughter that I would not stop searching until I posted 100 blessings on Facebook from this tragic event.

So please take time to enjoy 100 feel good moments that arose from the evacuation of 88,000 people…and this is just the beginning.

We are blessed.

The Blessings

1. The first person to reach out to me was an amazing friend that I had been trying to contact for 3 years!!

2. For all the times I complained about the cost of dance, driving back and forth all week to dance, travelling around the world for dance, it was because of DANCE that my daughter Ali and I were safe. We are blessed.

   We were already leaving for Calgary that day for a dance competition and had the car packed, full of gas and ready to go. I often reflect upon the residents that had only 10 minutes to pack knowing the severity of the wildfires.

3. The only things I need from my house are my family and our passports.

   As we fled from the smoke and flames, we did not know that there would soon be a full evacuation of Fort McMurray. My husband and son were still in our home when the mandatory evacuation was announced. I had time while driving down the highway to think about what they should try to save in our home. I thought about photos, family china, family jewelry, memory boxes of our children, our will and much much more. I scanned the house in my mind thinking about what they should try to save. I called my husband and asked him to please get the passports. In my time of reflection I realized that I was thinking about THINGS and what they meant to me. I did not need these things for the memories or to feel good. I really wanted my husband, son and dog to safely leave. I imagined everything else swallowed up by the fire and I was ok with that. I asked my dad in heaven to wrap his arms around my home and keep it safe for my return. Tears of enlightenment trickled down my cheeks...Joy comes from within.

1. To all friends and residents who lost their jobs and were struggling for work many new jobs will be created.

5. The overwhelming messages and support from family, friends, old school mates, former co-workers and acquaintances around the world.

6. The amazing fire fighters and workers who stayed behind to fight for our community.

7. Taxi drivers writing on their cabs FREE rides for Fort McMurray evacuees.

8. Hand written signs all over Alberta "we have food, we have a place for you to stay, stop in for a break, we have water, we have gas".

9. Bumping into a fellow resident at Market Mall, whom had lost her keys, lost her home, her phone had died, her hands were full and her eyes watering...I gave her my phone and my shoulder to cry on and a big hug. We are safe and we are blessed. We stand together!

10. Family time, pure and simple...

11. All of the volunteers and workers driving gas and supplies INTO the fire and the stranded vehicles on the side of the highway.

12. The Calgary radio station that stopped its call in to win broadcast and donated the $100,000 to Fort McMurray.

13. Volunteers from surrounding communities who acted so quickly to set up schools, sports complexes, community halls and more for Fort McMurray residents.

14. All residents safely evacuated as reported.

15. Friends and residents losing their home to foreclosure, a new beginning and a second chance.

16. Spending Mothers Day with my mom and my mother in law. A special blessing.

17. West Edmonton Mall opening its doors to Fort McMurray families for free entertainment.

18. Watching 2 young girls say with excitement, smiles and pure innocence "our school is burned down"!

19. Watching the tears of compassion roll down my daughter's cheeks as she received news that friends had lost their homes.

20. Hugging my son and husband who just made it to us. (Three days later)

21. Insight for so many people on what is important in life and what we can live without. Those who were blind now see. We are blessed.

    I have listened to a lot of people expressing the changes they are making in their lives since returning home. They are using more of their time to visit with friends and family. A beautiful shift in priorities.

22. The Calgary Flames and the Edmonton Oilers both donating $100,000!

23. The successful evacuation of the Northern Lights Hospital.

24. North Star Ford Calgary.

Volunteers immediately loaded semi trucks full of supplies at North Star Ford and sent them to Fort McMurray. The very giving nature of the owners, who as it turns out lost their family home in the fire and still continue to give generously in our community.

25. 2 healthy babies delivered at the evacuation camps!! Awesome blessings.

26. The amazing dance community. We arrived in Calgary for a dance competition. It soon turned in to a bake sale to raise funds for us along with water, food and snacks for Fort McMurray dancers

The Company that ran the dance competition donated all of the fees back to Generation Dance. Thank you. Another blessing.

27. The liquor store in Newfoundland donating the profits of their wine to Fort McMurray.

28. Fort McMurray residents rescuing pets and reuniting them with their owners.

29. My young nephew asking me "Auntie what happened to the forest animals are they ok?" What a different perspective.

30. Blessing #30 is our community!! No one, no fire can take that away! We stand together!!

31. Staying calm and rational as thousands and thousands of cars moved inch by inch over hours and hours fleeing a burning city, patience was a true blessing.

32. Expecting Grandparents in Edmonton were blessed when their daughter in law was flown in from Fort McMurray and gave birth shortly there after. They were overjoyed to be part of it.

33. Love...I have never felt so loved and so deeply loved and cared for as I do now as a Fort McMurray resident. I am so blessed. Thank you all

    An overall feeling resulting from how the whole evacuation was handled. Heartfelt messages, exhausted workers, donations, tears, laughter and humanity. People gave until they had nothing left to give. I am truly grateful for that.

34. Facebook and social media. With so many people worried about friends and family, the ability to post "SAFE" so quickly was a blessing.

35.   Bake sale from my hometown Maple Creek, Sask.!!!
       To raise funds for Fort McMurray.

It was truly unbelievable. From small towns to large cities across Canada and the world, everyone was doing what they could to help out. At this point on my blessings journey it wasn't just the raising of the funds that was incredible, it was the raising of our spirits. The warm and safe feeling I had knowing that millions of hands were reaching out to lift us up unconditionally…was a blessing. Thank you to everyone, you made a difference in our lives.

36. All of the schools around Alberta opening their doors to all of our students.

37. A distraught bride to be realized she forgot her dress behind. A bridal shop heard about it and opened up the whole store and told her to pick anything she wanted!

38. The Canadian Red Cross!!!!!!

   The International recognition of the Red Cross and the integrity of the organization was a huge asset during the wild fires. Donations from around the world poured in. When people didn't know where to go or whom to trust, they could contact the Red Cross. Residents were encouraged to register their name with them. This allowed concerned friends and family to locate loved ones. Gift card centers were set up to provide relief for food, clothing and accommodations. Shelters and necessity centers were quickly established to hand out donations of food, water, bedding and clothing. I have a much larger appreciation for the Red Cross and the help they provide people around the world in time of crisis. They continue to help the residents of Fort McMurray.

39. TD Meloche Monnex Insurance Company! Absolutely amazing service, very quick, full of compassion waived fees I could go on and on!! We are blessed!

10. Watching my daughters dance group in Calgary represent Fort McMurray in an emotional, heart felt, tearful dance ending with a standing ovation. Not a dry eye in the audience. Blessed with compassion.

11. WestJet! Safely evacuating not only people but pets as well! Imagine cats, dogs, guinea pigs, people and more all sitting on seats in the plane!!

    This amazing company surprised thousands of residents whom had lost their homes with a secret dinner gathering full of entertainment and surprises including trips around the world. Very uplifting in an emotional time.

12. Evacuating to Calgary. Helping out my distraught father in law who is exhausted. My mother in law has Alzheimer's and they were moving homes. I have patience to offer in a difficult situation. I am blessed to help out.

13. A friend of mine really wanted to renovate his home. He kept doing bits and pieces to fix it up. As he showed me the picture of it burnt he exclaimed, "Now I get a new home!!" Find your blessing, we all have them.

14. A mother reunited with her estranged daughter!! She had been trying for the past couple of years to reach out to her daughter who had "lost her way in

life". She couldn't make sense of it. Her daughter lost her home and is safe now with her mom. They found their blessing.

15. My brother in Minneapolis donating his Chiropractic clinic proceeds and services to Fort McMurray for 1 week!! We are blessed.

16. Finding your gift. I have searched for a long time to find my gift. It turns out I had it all the time, I just didn't know it. As we know gifts are for sharing. So if I have shared the gift of JOY in any of these posts I am truly blessed. "JOY comes from within"

17. Telus mobility waiving all texting and phone charges!!

18. Bootlegger 75% off along with multiple clothing stores!

19. Shoppers drug mart matching all points donated with cash! Plus 20% off in store.

20. 6 Calgary dancers stepped in to perform with Ali's dance group. They learned the choreography in a day!!! It was amazing!!!!!

Generous gifts of time and talent from these dancers was greatly appreciated. It was a stunning performance. They came together and danced as one.

51. Home made stands arose quickly to raise money for Fort McMurray and many people jumped in to donate their time and passion for the cause.

Facebook photo of students at Edge School Calgary raising money selling Gatorade and snacks to help Fort McMurray.

52. A resident had a flat tire a few days before the evacuation. The fire consumed his home while the car was safe at Canadian Tire.

53. A friend had her dog at an Edmonton kennel. Her home burnt along with dog bed, toys etc. The kennel surprised her with all new dog toys and bed!!!

54. The dance competition announced our last dance... With 28 dancers missing, the audience went wild with support, the energy was amazing tears were flowing, so much love and support!!! We are blessed!!!!! Thank you all.

55. Still waiting for blessing #55... Firefighters skinny dipping in my pool ;)!!

56. New friendships!! Strangers helping strangers and creating lifetime bonds.

57. A little boy in Toronto raised $2500 from a lemonade stand! What is his secret ingredient!!

    Comments: That's easy! LOVE is the boy's secret ingredient! :)

58. Amazing positive life lessons that my teenagers are learning, experiencing and witnessing. A true blessing, some things we just can't teach as parents…

59. Lac Labiche fire fighters handing out flowers to evacuee moms on Mother's Day.

60. Lac Labiche animal rescue shelter. They have saved and are caring for over 70 animals. You are blessed, your pet may be there safe and well cared for.

61. The teachers and principal from Good Shepard School in Fort McMurray. They safely evacuated all students while hot embers and flames fell all around them. Teachers stayed with all students until they all reunited with family members. For nearly 10 hours some waited with students, foregoing their own homes. We are blessed. We stand together.

62. There has not been 1 store in Calgary that I have gone into that doesn't have a sign up to support Fort McMurray! We are blessed!!

Join us for a
FREE COFFEE
and let's help
Fort Mac get back:

Donations accepted
at
Customer Service.

Thanks a tonne!

63. Thanking every clerk and cashier in person for the signs at their register. Telling them how grateful we all are. Their face soon turned to sympathy and compassion for all of Fort McMurray evacuees.

Our hearts are with those affected by the wildfires in Fort McMurray.

You can donate online via a link on the indigo.ca website which will connect you to the Canadian Red Cross webpage.

Thank you

61. Starbucks

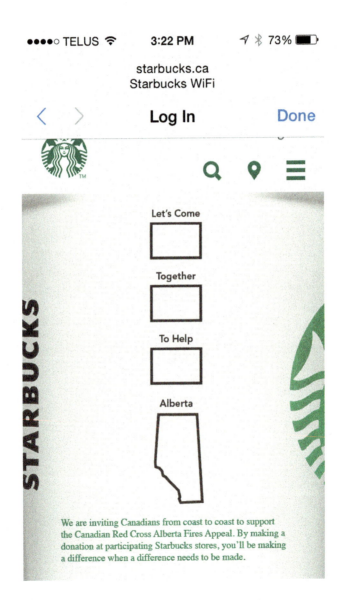

We are inviting Canadians from coast to coast to support the Canadian Red Cross Alberta Fires Appeal. By making a donation at participating Starbucks stores, you'll be making a difference when a difference needs to be made.

Facebook Mother's Day post from my Daughter:

Truly the most amazing person in my life, throughout all the current events you have managed to stay positive and help everyone around you from a lady in the mall who had also come from Fort Mac and needed a shoulder to cry on to compiling a list of 100 blessings that have come out of this. You are a light in the darkness to everyone in your life including myself, I am so grateful and appreciative to have someone like you to look up too and I don't say or show that nearly enough. You are a gift from god to this world, a true angel, Happy Mothers Day, I love you Joy Hepfner-Lalonde

65. Fire Chief Darby Allen. A real life hero... we are blessed.

   Darby Allen lead the battle against the Beast that had a mind of it's own. He was a pillar of strength, hope and reassurance during the desperate fight. He is humble, grateful and a positive role model. He had a job to do and he did it with honor. He reminded his team of their victories not their losses. He fought a hard battle and won.

66. Learning to Live in the Moment. Enjoy everyday. Today is a gift called The Present. Smile at everyone you see today! Listen to your children with your eyes. We have so many blessings.

67. Learning to live without...

When I posted this blessing I was thinking about all of the comforts from home that I was missing. Everything from my blender, ensuite bathroom, my sheets, bed and laptop computer. I now realize that the posting should have said, "learning to appreciate what you already have." I appreciate the freedom to do as I please in my home. I appreciate the comfort of home that I created. I was not learning to live without as much as I was appreciating what I had.

68. Evacuees loading trucks with supplies, helping out at shelters and jumping in with both feet to help out! For not focusing on what you lost but how you can help out!! You are a blessing and an inspiration!!

69. The Countries around the World offering their help and support!! We are blessed!! We stand together!

70. For all the awesome students of Fort McMurray, this one is for you... SCHOOL'S OUT FOR SUMMER!!!!!

71. Every cashier at Winners asked every customer at their till to donate ...and they did even if it was a dollar!! Thank you we are blessed.

72. Friends and family that we haven't seen for years tracking us down in Calgary! Inviting us to dinner, offering clothes, condos to stay in and so much more! I look forward to seeing you all!!!

73. Generation Dance Studio where Ali dances, waived our monthly payment $$! We are blessed!

74. My mother in law celebrating Mothers Day dinner with all of her children and all of her grandchildren. A beautiful blessing.

75. Toronto fire fighters prepared 1500 care packages for their Fort McMurray brothers saying 'we got your back'.

76. Flashing sign on Deerfoot Trail Calgary 'northern evacuees our home is your home'.

77. Humor!! Laughter is the best medicine. From the lady who packed cheese slices, to the husband who packed a bikini but no underwear for his wife and all the funny postings!! We are blessed with laughter!!

78. Recognition!!

    Facebook photo newspaper clipping that says, "...What's been developed in and around Fort McMurray has been a blessing, not a curse, to this province and this country. As we rebuild and recover, we mustn't forget that."

I felt like I was finally not alone, looking for all of the good in this situation.

79. Wandering River Lodge. The quick action taken by the camp's supervisor and generosity of the owner they soon transformed the lodge into an evacuation center! They offered 3 free hot meals a day and focused on setting up games and distractions for children and families. We are blessed!

80. Everything that is still standing and was not consumed by the fire!!!! We are blessed.

81. Crisis centers being set up to help people cope and provide emotional support. We are blessed. We stand together!

82. A home was burnt to the ground, the memorial of a loved one in the yard ...untouched the only thing left standing…

83. A grade 6 evacuee was interviewed about starting a new school. She said everyone was so nice and welcoming and how great it was that now her best friend was in her class! A blessing for her.

84. High schools offering to arrange Graduations!! Plus grads looking for their "plus 1" from Fort McMurray students !!;)

85. Amazing blessing!

Facebook photo newspaper clip:

"Welcome Fort McMurray evacuees. As a community, we are dedicated to assisting our friends and neighbors to the north. We welcome you to Strathcona County, and while you are not here under ideal conditions, we will do our best to meet your social, physical and emotional needs.

While you are here, you are welcome to access all County recreation facilities, along with local and commuter transit service, free of charge. This includes a convenient shuttle to take you to the places that will be of most value to you. You will find a link to recreation activities and transit schedules on our website.

You are also welcome to access computers and Internet in the library, located in our Community Centre.

Our family and Community Services staff are also available to help you with local support services. Please stop in to talk to them, or call local support for programs and services 780-464-4044.

A listing of some of the resources available to you is included on the back of this flyer. More resources and information can be found at www.strathcona.ca/ FortMacFire.

Please know our community is here for you and your family.

Roxanne Carr, Mayor"

86. A father and his daughter were reunited with their dog 1 week after the fire. Their home was destroyed. They were not able to rescue their pet. They have no idea how their dog was rescued. What a beautiful blessing!

87. The dress shop in Camrose offering FREE grad dresses to Fort McMurray Grads! We are blessed!

88. High River flood evacuees, with their own natural disaster still fresh, bought and delivered gift cards to Northern evacuees. They also signed up to come clean up Fort McMurray. We are blessed!

89. While a school was being evacuated, a young girl called her dad about the fire and sent him to wake up her brother who had come off night shift.

    Their home burnt to the ground... No casualties What a blessing!

90. Twinning of highway 63. The only road out of Fort McMurray...

91. TIME! Start checking off your "time" list!!

    I don't have time to workout
    I don't have time to read
    I don't have time to visit
    I don't have time to write the book I want to write

    I don't have time to look for a new job that I enjoy

    I don't have time to learn/try something new

    If I only had more TIME...
    Enjoy your TIME!! We are blessed!!

92. Acts of Random Kindness! All evacuees that I have had the pleasure to speak with have astounding stories of Acts of Random Kindness. The only tears I have seen so far are not from loss or sadness but from the overwhelming acts of humanity.

    We are blessed.

93. The realization that there really is...
    No place like HOME...
    We are blessed

94. Patience...

    Inch by inch and hour upon hour vehicles evacuated a burning city. Line ups at camps, line ups for gas, line-ups for gift cards, line-ups at evacuation centers and more we were blessed with patience. 88,000 people displaced waiting to hear when they can return home. Remember blessing 94, we are blessed with Patience.

95. Exhausted Fire fighters and rescue workers reuniting with families for some R and R. Enjoy! We are blessed

I have tried to imagine myself in their shoes. Families separated by the ravaging wildfire. As a wife would I feel proud or scared for my exhausted husband giving everything he could to save our community. As a husband and father would knowing that I gave my all to Fort McMurray in a crisis ease the time away from family? Regardless, you are all heroes. You are all blessings.

96. Finding Inner Strength.

Saving a pet from a burning home, parents staying calm to evacuate children, saying goodbye to loved ones who stayed behind to battle the blaze, sleeping in a row of cots with thousands of strangers, living out of a suitcase indefinitely, trying to save a strangers home while yours burnt to the ground. This fire is proof ...we all have inner strength. We are blessed. We stand together.

97. Getting out of our comfort zone and trying something new!

As days turn into weeks of evacuation and uncertainty our comfort zone is tested.

New hairdressers, new doctors, new dentists, new teachers. Change is good try something NEW today!!

Try a new class, try a new restaurant, try a new sport, and try something NEW today!! You just might like it!!! We are safe… We are blessed.

98. The Giving Hasn't Stopped!

Pub nights are being organized, concerts and dance shows are booked all in an effort to keep on giving. As we grow tired and anxious and want to give up remember that NO ONE has given up on us!!!! We are blessed. We stand together.

Shanks Calgary photo on Facebook:

＊ Still waiting for Blessing #55!

This was my wishful thinking and humor that Fire Fighters would be skinny-dipping in my outdoor pool. Cheers!

99. The Many Blessings Still to Come!! Watch for them!!

5,10,15 years from now we will look back and say if it wasn't for this tragedy we would not be WHERE we are or WHO we are today.

Alberta Strong
Canada Strong
World Wide Strong
We are blessed .

We stand together!

Well as tears of Joy drip on my phone, I am proud to post Blessing #100...

When the smoke has cleared and the ashes have settled blessing #100 will emerge.

100. A NEW BEGINNING

Follow your dreams. We will come back stronger and more beautiful than ever!! We are and always will be blessed! Thank you all :)

In closing I would like to leave you with this…

❤️ *Enjoy life nothing is certain*

❤️ *Look in the mirror every day and like what you see*

❤️ *Blessings are everywhere!!!*

❤️ *Words do not teach at all,*
it is life experience that brings wisdom

❤️ *You already have everything you need*

❤️ *When you feel that life has you down,*
open this book to any page and find joy

❤️ *The fire in our hearts burns brighter*
than any wild fire #fortmacstrong

❤️ *All events in life are blessings given*
to us to learn and grow from.

❤️ *Accept the things you can not change*

❤️ *Fill your day with love*

❤️ *Say less do more*

The evacuation of Fort McMurray
during the wild fire has been…
The Greatest Gift

💜 *Joy Comes From within*

Thank you all for sharing.

Afterthought

The publishing of "the Greatest Gift" has been a journey filled with self -discovery, enlightenment and empowerment. Filled with breakdowns, breakthroughs and fear turning into courage.

In my deepest darkest hour I turned to a deck of cards that my kids gave me a few years ago. On the cover it said "52 things we love about you". I opened it to number 35. It said "we love how you always see the best in the worst situations". I cried and cried and cried and through the tears I pressed, "enter" and sent in my manuscript for "The Greatest Gift".

Thanks again to the incredible staff at Friesen Press including Ellie Moller for being my rock, believing in me and guiding me to inner JOY.

I would love to hear from you.
Please email me your blessings.

todayichoosejoy.lalonde@gmail.com

CPSIA information can be obtained
at www.ICGtesting.com
Printed in the USA
LVOW06s1345230517
535199LV00003B/4/P